STOCK TRADING FOR A LIVING

How to Make Money and Become Financially Free by Investing in the Stock Market With This Comprehensive Trading Guide (2022 Crash Course for Beginners)

Ivor Clarke

CONTENTS

INTRODUCTION TO STOCK TRADING

Not everyone who buys and sells stocks is a stock trader, at least in the nuanced language of investment terms. Depending on how often they buy and sell stocks, most fall into one of two camps: traders or investors.

The cartoon of the trader is that of the frenzied Wall Streeter in front of scrolling monitors and tickers, buying and selling throughout the day. Investors, on the other hand, tend to participate for the long term, buying at regular intervals and selling much less often, or not at all, at least until retirement.

However, stock trading isn't always what you see on the floor of the New York Stock Exchange, and it's possible to get started from the comfort of your couch. But you better know what you are doing before doing your first trade.

What is stock trading?

Stock traders buy and sell stocks to capitalize on daily price fluctuations. These short-term traders are betting that they can make a few bucks in the next minute, hour, day, or month, rather than buying stock in a top-of-the-line company to hold for years or even decades.

There are two main types of stock trading:

Active trading is what an investor does who performs 10 or more trades per month. They typically use a strategy that relies heavily on market timing, trying to take advantage of short-term events (at the company level or based on market fluctuations) to make a profit in the next few weeks or months.

Intraday trading is the strategy employed by investors who play with stocks: buying, selling and closing their positions in the same stock in a single trading day, without much concern about the internal workings of the underlying businesses. (Position refers to the amount of a particular stock or fund you own.) The daily trader's goal is to earn a few dollars in the next few minutes, hours, or days based on daily price fluctuations.

HOW TO TRADE STOCKS

If you are trying your hand at trading stocks for the first time, know that most investors will benefit best if they keep things simple and invest in a diversified mix of low-cost index funds to achieve, and this is key, superior returns. long-term. That said, the logistics of trading stocks comes down to six steps:

1. Open a brokerage account

Trading stocks requires funding a brokerage account, a specific type of account designed to hold investments. If you don't have an account yet, you can open one with an online broker in a few minutes. But don't worry, opening an account doesn't mean you're investing your money just yet. It just gives you the option to do it once you are ready.

2. Establish a stock trading budget

Even if you find a talent for trading stocks, allocating more than 10% of your portfolio to individual stocks can expose your savings to too much volatility. But this is not the only rule for managing risk. Other dos and don'ts include:

> Invest only as much money as you can afford to lose. Do not use money for short-term expenses that you must pay, such as a down payment or tuition.

> Cut that 10% if you don't already have a healthy emergency fund and 10-15% of your income goes into a retirement savings account.

3. Learn how to use market orders and limit orders

Once you have your brokerage account and budget in place, you can use your online broker's website or trading platform to place your stock trades. You will be presented with several options for the types of orders, which dictate how your trade is performed. We go through them in detail in our guide on how to buy stocks, but these are the two most common types:

Market order: buy or sell the shares as soon as possible at the best available price.

Limit order: buy or sell the shares only at a specific price or better than the established one. For a buy order, the limit price will be the maximum you are willing to pay and the order will be approved only if the share price falls to or below that amount.

4. Practice with a virtual business account

There is nothing better than a low-pressure, hands-on experience, which investors can gain through the virtual trading tools offered by many online brokers. Paper trading allows clients to test their business acumen and build a track record before putting real dollars at stake.

5. Measure your returns against a suitable benchmark.

This is essential advice for all types of investors, not just assets. The ultimate goal in choosing stocks is to be ahead of a benchmark. That could be the Standard & Poor's 500 Index (often used as a substitute for "the market"), the Nasdaq Composite Index (for those who invest primarily in tech stocks), or other smaller indices that are made up of companies based on size, industry and geography.

Measuring results is key, and if a serious investor cannot outperform the benchmark (something even professional investors struggle to do), then it makes financial sense to invest in a low-cost index mutual fund or ETF, essentially a basket of stocks whose performance closely aligns with that of one of the benchmark indices.

6. Keep your perspective

Being a successful investor doesn't require finding the next big breakout action before everyone else. By the time you hear that XYZ stocks are poised for a jump, so have thousands of professional traders and the potential has likely already been included in the stock price. It may be too late to make a quick profit, but that doesn't mean it's too late for the party. Truly great investments continue to provide shareholder value for years, which makes a good case for treating active investing as a hobby rather than a Hail Mary for quick riches.

How To Survive Stock Trading

Wherever you are on the investor-trader spectrum, these four tips on how to trade stocks can help ensure you do so safely.

1. Reduce risk by building positions gradually

There is no need to shoot down with any position. Taking your time to buy (through dollar cost averaging or buying in thirds) helps reduce investor exposure to price volatility.

2. Ignore the "cool tips"

WallStreetHotShot4721 on the EZMillion $ Trade forum and the people who pay for sponsored ads promoting safe stocks are not your genuine Wall Street friends, mentors, or gurus. In many cases, they are part of a pump-and-dump racket in which suspicious people buy buckets of stock in a little-known and little-traded company (often a penny stock) and go online to promote it.

As unwitting investors load up the shares and increase the price, criminals take their profits, throw away their shares, and put them back on the ground. Don't help them fill their pockets. If you're looking for a guru, bookmark Warren Buffett's annual letters to shareholders for common-sense advice and observations on sensible long-term investing.

3. Keep good records for the IRS

If you're not using an account that has favored tax status, such as a 401 (k) or other workplace accounts, or a Roth account or traditional IRA, taxes on investment gains and losses can get complicated.

The IRS applies different rules and tax rates and requires the filing of different forms for different types of merchants. Another benefit of keeping good records is that losing investments can be used to offset income taxes paid through a neat strategy called tax loss collection.

4. Choose your broker wisely

To trade stocks, you need a broker, but don't be fooled by any broker. Choose one with the terms and tools that best suit your investing style and experience. A higher priority for active traders will be low commissions and fast order execution for urgent trades. See our picks of the best online platforms for active traders / daily traders for more information.

Investors who are new to trading should look for a broker who can teach them the tools of the trade through educational articles, online tutorials, and in-person seminars (check out NerdWallet's recaps for the best brokers for beginners). Other features to consider are the quality and availability of stock picking and analysis tools, on-the-fly alerts, easy order entry, and customer service.

Whatever happens, the time spent learning the fundamentals of how to research stocks and experiencing the ups and downs of stock trading, even if there are more of the latter, is time well spent, as long as you are enjoying the journey not putting money down that can't afford to lose on the line.

STOCK TRADING FAQ

Which Stock Trading Site Is Best For Beginners?

NerdWallet has reviewed and ranked online stockbrokers based on which ones are the best for beginners. This list takes into consideration the broker's investment selection, customer support, account fees, account minimum, trading costs, and more.

What is a good stock trading strategy for beginners?

Practice with a virtual trading account first, then start by investing low amounts to avoid unnecessary risk. From here, you can gradually increase the amount, but remember: don't invest anything you can't afford to lose, and keep your exposure to individual stocks at 10% of your portfolio.

Can you trade stocks with $ 100?

Yes, as long as the share price is less than $ 100 and your brokerage account does not have any required minimums or fees that could push the transaction to more than $ 100. The best online brokers for beginners will have no minimums or fees, so with them, you'll be ready to invest $ 100 in any company whose stock price is $ 100 or less. Some brokers also allow you to buy fractional shares, which means that you can buy a portion of a share if you cannot pay the full price of the share.

What is the difference between stock trading and investing?

The main difference is how often you buy and sell stocks. Traders buy and sell more frequently, while investors tend to buy and hold for the long term. Learn more about stock trading vs. investing here.

What time can I start trading in the day?

Normal trading hours on the New York Stock Exchange and the Nasdaq are 9:30 am to 4 pm ET on non-holiday business days. However, there are also pre-market and after-hours sessions; Not all brokers allow you to trade during these extended market hours, but many do.

WHAT IS THE STOCK MARKET AND HOW DOES IT WORK

Currently there are many people who think that the **stock market** is only a high risk place, where if you do not have money, you will lose everything; And this is something totally false, since there are thousands of cases of people who have arrived with little and have managed to multiply their capital; In the same way, there are many cases of people who have gone from having millions to nothing, in a matter of months, therefore, it is important to know that yes, you can make money with little, but also, you can lose a lot in very Little time.

Taking into account the aforementioned, it is important to **know that the stock market is not a unique entity,** since there is one in each country (or in most of them) and depending on the country where you are, some things may change, for example:

- The ease of buying and selling stocks.

- Assets that are listed on the stock market.

- The requirements to make a company go public.

- The laws and / or entities that regulate it.

- The requirements that are required to trade in it.

Now, the **general operation of the stock exchanges** (some aspects may change depending on the stock market, but it is almost always the same), is as follows: when creating a company, you have the option of dividing it into shares, with The objective that one or more people can acquire a part of it, in this way, they obtain dividends (part of the total earnings) and also, if the shares are revalued, it means a higher profitability for the owners of the shares.

Now, **when a company is growing rapidly, you have the option of going public**, that is; place a number of **shares for sale on the stock market**, so that independent investors (and everyone in general) can buy a percentage of the company; This makes the value of the company go up or down, depending on supply and demand.

The value of the shares will depend on the people who want to buy the shares and who want to sell it, if the number of people interested in buying is greater, this translates into an increase in the value of the shares, since the shareholders will ask for more money for the shares, and the opposite will happen, if the number of people interested in buying is less than those interested in selling; since the shareholders will have to set lower prices, in order to be able to sell the shares and get out of them.

What is AT in the stock market (Technical Analysis)

AT, refers to technical analysis, which is a study that serves to evaluate the market action, that is; know how the market will act, through a series of graphs, which in turn, take into account the following factors:

- **Asset price**.

- **Stock market volume**. This is equal to the number of contracts that have been closed on an asset.

- **Open interest**. It is normally used in future markets. It basically tries to evaluate the number of contracts that exist without closing, before the end of the period.

The TA (technical analysis) is normally displayed graphically, showing the three factors mentioned above; This allows a quick evaluation of a specific market or asset, in order to try to predict the ups or downs that it may suffer.

It is important to mention that one of the most relevant factors in this study is the stock market volume, since this factor allows us to know the demand and supply of an asset, therefore, depending on the result, it can be known what will happen with the price of an asset in a certain period of time (if demand is high, the value will tend to rise and quite the opposite if demand is low and supply is high).

Finally, it is essential to note that this analysis is not exact, that is, it does not guarantee the results, and that it only studies the behavior of the price and nothing else. Since the Price contains all the behaviors and interpretations of the market of the different participants.

What is AF in the stock market (Fundamental Analysis)

AF means fundamental analysis and it can be said that it is one of the main study techniques used when trying to predict the value of an asset, and this is mainly due to the fact that this study is responsible for knowing the commercial and real value of an asset.

In short, it is responsible for knowing the real value of an asset, beyond its listing on the stock market, therefore, it serves to detect financial bubbles or assets that may increase their value exponentially over time.

On the other hand, it should be noted that this type of analysis is quite complex and deep, because it takes into account a large number of factors, such as:

- Study of the company itself.

- Study of the products that the company sells.

- It takes into account the strategies that the company plans or is applying.

- Political and legal situation of the company; In addition, it also studies its products (for example, if a food company has controversy regarding the quality of its products, this may be a factor that causes the value to go down, therefore, it is something that is taken into account) .

- Situations that may favor or harm the company and its products (such as: laws, control over prices, rejection or social acceptance, among other things).

As such, **the Fundamental Analysis studies everything related to the factors that can intervene in the company's earnings** and therefore, in the value of its shares, as a result of this, it is usually a fairly accurate analysis, although sometimes, A surprise factor may appear or not taken into account, which may create variations in what is expected, that is, there may be a factor and / or event that intervenes and generates an unexpected result.

Difference between AT and AF

It is important to understand that although both analyzes seek the same thing (trying to predict the price of an asset), they are not the same and have considerable differences, among which we can mention:

- The technical analysis only evaluates the behavior of the price, that is, it does not take into account at any time, the external factors that may affect the value of the asset. On the other hand, fundamental analysis studies all the factors that can affect the price of the asset and although it takes into account the market, it is not really the predominant factor.

- The fundamental analysis seeks to predict the price, but it does not predict the time in which said prediction will be fulfilled, that is, this analysis can say that the shares of a company will rise, but it does not indicate how long it will happen. On the other hand, technical analysis can be applied to predict the price of an asset in the short term.

- Fundamental analysis is more rudimentary, that is, its techniques are more study and general analysis, however, technical analysis is not, since it is based on numbers to predict market behavior.

Both analyzes are fundamental and used by many traders, however, it is always best to do a combination of both techniques, in this way, you can predict the behavior of an asset in the short, medium and long term. Although as mentioned above, it is important to note that these analyzes are not always accurate and the end result may not be what you expected.

Financial products and their relationship with the stock market

There are many financial products that, in one way or another, are linked to the stock market and among the most popular we can mention the following:

The actions

Actions are the parts in which an organization is divided (companies, companies, etc.). Whoever has the greatest number of shares will have greater influence over the organization, because, in a certain way, they will own it, that is, if a shareholder owns all the shares of a company, he or she becomes the owner of the same. The same occurs if the shareholder owns more than 51% of the shares.

On many occasions the shares of an organization can be traded on stock exchanges, but this is not always the case. When a stock is publicly traded, it can generate a series of contracts and derivatives, which are used in other markets, to produce profits for people with less capital than is necessary to buy a company's stock.

In conclusion, stocks are the basis for a wide variety of markets and it can be said that they are the mainstay of much of the world economy.

Futures

Future contracts are those in which two parties establish the price and date of purchase of a certain asset . When the expiration date (that is, the date on which the negotiation will take place), both parties must comply with what is established in the contract and one of the two parties may win more than the other, depending on the asset price variation.

In conclusion: if an asset rises in price and exceeds the purchase value, this will mean that the buyer will win and the seller will lose; if the opposite happens, this will mean profits for the seller and losses for the buyer.

It is important to mention that there is a whole market for future contracts, where these contracts are bought and sold, which always represent an asset, therefore, its value is subject to its behavior.

Options

Options are financial derivatives and basically, it deals with the right granted to the buyer to acquire an asset and the obligation of a holder to sell it, as a result of a previously established contract.

Namely; A contract is established, where the price and the date of the negotiation are agreed, on that date, the buyer will have the right, but not the obligation, to acquire the asset, however, the seller will have the obligation to sell it (at least that the buyer does not want to carry out the transaction, in that case, the owner of the asset will keep it and in return, receive a guarantee, established at the time of making the contract).

It is worth mentioning that to guarantee the fulfillment of the contract, it is normally carried out with an intermediary, who is in charge of requesting guarantees from both parties.

ETF (Exchange Traded Fund)

This name is given due to its acronym in English (Exchange Traded Fund) and they are investment funds, which are usually listed on the stock market, therefore, the shareholder (or participant), buys shares of the fund, instead of acquiring a share of the The same, that is, they are larger, more stable and guaranteed investment funds.

The main reason why investment funds decide to do this is that by going public, it generates greater confidence in investors, because this means that it is regulated by all the laws of the country where the asset is registered. background.

Investment funds and their relationship with the stock market

Investment funds are organizations that are responsible for receiving money from different people (called savers), to later proceed to invest it in financial products, all with the aim of generating profitability and benefiting all fund participants.

When a person invests a capital within an investment fund, it is necessary to understand that it will be the organizers of the same who will be in charge of managing said money, that is; the owner of the capital will not have control over what is done with it, since it is the organizers who are in charge of evaluating the situation.

Normally the organizers (or managers), are in charge of evaluating the market, to determine which are the safest and most profitable investments that can be made, because their main objective is to generate profitability, more, it does not matter if it is slow (since they must keep the savers who participate in the fund happy, to avoid that they withdraw their capital and therefore generate stability problems).

The profitability for each saver will depend on the amount that belongs to the fund, that is; that the more money is invested in it, the higher profits it will get from time to time, as long as the fund's profitability is positive.

Investment funds are usually born from the need to carry out large stock movements, with the aim of having greater profitability, but without risking much, that is to say; When many people make up an investment fund, it has a large capital to invest, however, those who make up the fund have not placed huge amounts of money, therefore, the risk in a certain way is lower, since if something goes wrong, the amount risked is less than it would be if it were invested alone.

The only problem with investment funds is the low profits that can be obtained annually, however, it is a good way to put savings to work, since, relatively speaking, it is safe (as long as the investment fund has a good reputation and is managed by true experts).

Finally, it is necessary to emphasize that **investment funds** sometimes **play an important role in the stock market**, since some funds handle huge amounts of money and therefore, what they do can generate effects in the market, since that if they sell a large number of shares of a certain company, this can cause the demand for it to drop and therefore; its value. On the other hand, mutual funds can sometimes be publicly traded, as mentioned above.

TYPES OF STOCK TRADING

The main Stock Trading types are:

1. Common stock and preferred stock

Concerning the rights that the shareholder receives, a distinction can be made between **ordinary shares** and **preference shares**. When you purchase a common share, you also have a vote at the general meeting. You can therefore participate in the decisions of the company management or use your veto. Preference shares do not allow you to vote; you will usually receive more dividends as compensation. The ordinary shareholder will therefore prefer preference shares.

2. Bearer shares and registered shares

Another distinction is made according to the transferability of the shares. The rights from a bearer share belong to the holder, i.e. the one who owns the paper. In the case of registered shares, however, the name of the shareholder must be entered in the share register. Most of the stocks you will purchase are bearer stocks.

3. Par value and no-par shares

In the case of nominal value shares, the share capital of the shares is divided according to the nominal value of the shares. Often the face value is € 1 so that a corresponding number of shares are issued. No-par shares have no par value. In this case, only the number of shares is specified in the articles of association of the stock corporation.

4. Young and old stocks

New shares are offered to shareholders in the event of a capital increase. If a company needs more money, it can do a capital increase. Then more shares are issued to raise more money. Old stocks, on the other hand, are stocks that were already available before the capital increase. The holders of old shares receive subscription rights as compensation, which they can

either use to buy new shares or sell them on the stock
exchange like shares.

TERMS IN STOCK TRADING

Open price: the price at which the shares are first traded after the day's opening. If there is no closing price within 30 minutes of the market opening, the price of closing of the previous days is considered the opening price. Every day when the market opens, stocks open at a specific price, called the opening price. Stock prices are constantly moving throughout the trading day as supply and demand for stocks change.

Closing price: the price of the last share traded each day, that is, the closing price. It is the last level an asset was traded at before the market closed on a given day. Closing prices are often used as a marker when looking at long-term movements. They can be compared to previous closing prices or to the opening price to measure the movement of an asset in a single day.

Some financial assets are only traded during certain hours of the day. Stocks and indices, for example, traditionally can only be traded while their financial markets are open. Until those assets are marketable again, their closing prices are the most current level for the asset. The closing price can be higher or lower than the opening price, depending on the market sentiment that day.

Highest Price: The highest price among the prices negotiated on that day; sometimes the highest price is only one, sometimes more than one.

Lowest Price: The lowest price among the prices negotiated on that day; sometimes the lowest price is only one, sometimes more than one.

High-performing stocks: stocks of companies that have performed well but have experienced slower growth. These companies have the strength to withstand the recession, but they cannot bring you exciting profits. mature and they don't need to spend a lot of money to expand their business, investing in these companies is primarily focused on getting dividends, and when you invest in this kind of stocks, the P ratio / e is not too high, but you should also take into account the historical volatility of stock prices during an economic downturn.

Hot Stock: These are stocks with high trading volume, high liquidity, and stock prices change dramatically.

Growth stocks: The stocks issued by those companies whose sales and profits continue to grow faster than the country and the industry as a whole. These companies generally have high ambition, focus on scientific research, and have significant profits to be reinvested to stimulate their expansion.

Volume: reflects the volume of transactions. In general, it can be measured by the number of shares traded and the amount of the transaction. At present, both stock market indicators of Shenzhen and Shanghai can be displayed.

Price: the unit of increase or decrease in price. The price level varies according to the market value of each share. Take the example of the Shanghai Stock Exchange: the price of 100 RMB at the end of the market per share is 0.10 RMB, the price of 100 - 200 RMB per share is 0.20 RMB, the price of 200 - 300 RMB is 0.30 RMB, the price of 300 - 400 RMB per share is 0, 50 RMB, the price of 400 RMB or more is 1.00 RMB.

Suspension: The exchange suspends the trading of shares in the stock market due to a continuous rise or falls in the price of the shares due to new or activity. Once the situation is clarified or as the business returned to normal, it resumed trading on the stock exchange.

Rise or Fall: Each day's closing price is compared to the previous day's closing price to determine whether the stock price is rising or falling. Typically, notice boards above the Trading Desk are marked with a "+" - "sign.

Increase (decrease) in closing value: the maximum value of the increase (decrease) in the price of the shares specified by the exchange during a day is the percentage of the closing price of the previous day, which cannot be exceeded, otherwise the negotiation will be automatically stopped.

Rise: the opening price is much higher than the previous day's closing price.

Open at a low price: The open price is much lower than the previous day's closing price.

Quotation: This means that investors do not actively buy or sell and often adopt a wait-and-see attitude, causing the stock price to change very little on this day, which is called quotation.

Short jump: This is a large jump in the stock price that is spurred on by strong positive or negative news. Short jumps usually occur before the start or end of a large movement in the stock price.

Capital market: the capital market refers to the financial market for the financing of securities and medium and long-term capital loans of a duration of more than one year. The money market is the financial market that manages the facility. short-term financing within one year. Fund seekers raise long-term funds through the capital market and short-term funds through the money market.

Shares: shares are share certificates issued by a public limited company to investors when raising capital and represent the ownership of its holders in the joint-stock company. It has the following basic characteristics: non - redemption, participation, return (stocks are generally preferred by investors in times of high inflation), liquidity, price volatility, and risk. Shares are one of the most widespread instruments of financial markets. They represent a portion of the capital stock of the company and make whoever acquires them a shareholder or partner of the same.

The shares are the equal parts in which the <u>capital stock</u> of a <u>public limited company</u> is divided. These parts are owned by a person, who is called a **shareholder**, and represent the ownership that the person has in the company, that is, the percentage of the company that belongs to the shareholder. Owning shares in a company confers legitimacy on the shareholder to demand their rights and fulfill their obligations. Among other rights, we can mention: to vote in the Shareholders' Meeting, to demand information on the situation of <u>the company</u>, or to sell the shares it owns. Among other obligations, the shareholder will also have to bear the losses, if during a period the company does not obtain good results.

Bonds: Bonds are debt securities issued to investors by the Government, financial institutions, industrial and commercial enterprises, and other institutions that directly raise funds from social loans and promise to pay interest to a company. It determines the interest rate and repays the principal on the agreed terms. It has the following characteristics: repayment, liquidity, security, and profitability. Normally, when we have to borrow money, individuals go to a credit institution (a bank). In this case, a loan agreement or some type of credit is formalized, however, there is a single lender and a single borrower.

But this does not mean that it is the only way to go into debt to get financing. It is possible to borrow money from the general public, issuing debt in droves that will be bought by people interested in investing.

These investors must be paid a certain interest rate for lending us the money. In these cases, some documents are issued (in reality they are usually simple accounting entries, they are not physical documents) in which it is recognized that they have lent us a certain amount of money. The title itself specifies what **annual interest** is paid to investors/lenders and when the loan matures (the duration of the bond expires). The periodic interest paid is what is known as a coupon.

Convertible Securities: These are a type of securities that holders have the right to convert into another type of securities of a different nature, mainly including convertible corporate bonds and convertible preferred shares.

Warrants: securities issued by the issuer of index securities or by a third party other than this, of which the agreed holder has the right to buy or sell the underlying securities to the issuer at a price agreed upon in the index. a specified time or on a specified due date, or to collect the settlement difference utilizing a Cash Settlement. when issued by the issuer, agreed holders have the right to purchase underlying securities from the issuer at an agreed price within a specified time frame or on specified maturity date.

Sales mandate: when issued by the issuer, the agreed holder has the right to sell the underlying securities to the issuer at the agreed price within a specified time frame or on specific maturity date.

An investment fund in transferable securities: the Fund designates a mode of collective investment in transferable securities in which the interests and risks are shared, i.e. the funds of the investors are centralized by the issue. fund units, placed in the custody of the Fund's custodian, managed and used by the Fund manager to invest in financial instruments such as stocks and bonds.

Open-ended funds: funds for which the total issue amount is not fixed and for which the total number of fund units is increased or decreased at any time, and for which investors can subscribe or redeem shares. fund units in places of business designated by the State based on the Fund's rating.

Closed fund: this is a fund whose total issue amount is determined in advance and whose total number of fund units remains unchanged during the closed period. After the Fund has been listed, investors can transfer and buy fund units through the securities market.

Primary market: the primary market for shares, i.e. the issue market, on which investors can subscribe for shares issued by the company.

The full name of IPO designates the method of issuing the initial public offering of a company (public limited company or limited liability company) to the public.

Issue price: when a share is listed and issued, the listed company, from the point of view of the personal interest of the company and the guarantee of the success of the listing of the shares, issues the listed shares not. at face value, but sets a more reasonable price for the issue, which is called the issue price of the shares.

Premium offer: means the public offer of a newly listed company at a price higher than the nominal value or the cash capital increase of a listed company at a price higher than the nominal value.

Discount issue: Issue at a price lower than the previous price.

Secondary market: the circulation market, which is the place where the issued shares are traded.

Shares: The official name of shares is RMB ordinary shares.

B shares: The official name of B shares is RMB special shares.

H shares: H shares are foreign shares registered on the mainland and listed in Hong Kong.

S shares: Shanghai and Shenzhen Stock Exchange adjusts after the abbreviation of shares. Among them, 1014 companies g canceled the "g" marking and reinstated the abbreviation of the shares before the implementation of the plan. share reform; the other 276 companies which have not reformed shares or which have reformed shares but have not yet reformed shares have been marked "s" before the abbreviation to warn investors.

ST shares: St sector shares refer to shares listed on the Shanghai and Shenzhen stock markets. Due to operating losses or other abnormal circumstances, csrc intends to draw the attention of shareholders to, especially traded shares.

ST shares: St sector shares refer to shares listed on the Shanghai and Shenzhen stock markets. For individual stocks at risk of going public, the China Securities Regulatory Commission (csrc) intends to draw the attention of shareholders to stocks that are subject to special treatment.

Blue chips: Blue chips are shares issued by listed companies with abundant capital, equity, and a large market capitalization.

Red chips: Red chips are those stocks with the Concept of China Mainland that Hong Kong and International Investors will Register outside China and listed in Hong Kong.

Stocks with good results: these are stocks with good results and surpluses in recent years, which can still be optimistic in the years to come, except that there will be no growth The outlook for the industry is good and the return on investment can be maintained at a certain level.

Waste inventory: Waste inventory is the inventory of a company with poor performance. Some of these companies have even entered the category of losses due to poor industrial prospects or poor management. of its stocks in the market is low, stock prices are falling, trading is not active, and year-end dividends are low.

Growth Stock: This is the corporate stock with a higher rate of profit growth in new and promising industries. The stock prices of growth stocks tend to rise.

Cold Door shares: stock with small Trading volume, Poor circulatory and Small Price change.

Leading stocks: Leading stocks are those which have influence and appeal over other stocks of the same industry in stock market speculation at a certain period. Their fluctuations tend to guide and demonstrate the fluctuations of stocks in other industries. Leader stock is not static, its status can often only last for a certain time.

State shares: State shares refer to the shares formed by the ministries or bodies authorized to invest on behalf of the State (SASAC) by investing in the company with assets belonging to the State, including shares converted into existing state-owned assets of the company. It is an integral part of the state's participation.

Shares of legal entities: shares of legal entities refer to shares that are not listed on the stock exchange and which circulate in the company as legal entities of companies or public institutions and social organizations endowed with personality. legal and who are invested in the company with their legally available assets.

Public stocks: Public stocks are those stocks that can be listed and distributed when the social public invests in the company with the assets it owns following the law.

Fundamentals: Fundamentals include the macroeconomic situation and the basic situation of listed companies. The macroeconomic situation reflects the overall performance of listed companies and sets the context for the further development of listed companies. Therefore, macroeconomics is closely related to listed companies and corresponding stock prices. The basic bread of listed companies includes financial position, profit situation, market share, management system, the composition of talents, etc.

Technical aspect: The technical aspect refers to the technical index, the trend shape, and the combination of Klines reflecting the dielectric change. Technical analysis is based on three assumptions, namely that the behavior of the market contains all information, that prices change with a certain trend or regularity and history repeats itself. As market behavior includes all information, macroeconomic and political factors can be ignored, and changes in market Prices are regular and as history will repeat itself, it is easy to judge the future trend from historical transaction data.

Bull market: The bull market is also known as the bull market, which means that the bull market is generally bullish and has a long duration.

Bear market: Also known as the short market, the bear market refers to a sharply declining market with a relatively long duration.

BROKERS

To buy shares (or sell them) you need a **broker to** do it for you. A broker is a person (or a company) who is authorized to buy and sell shares on the market. You tell him what and how much you want to buy or sell and he does it to you, in exchange for a small commission. To operate, it requires the authorization of the respective regulatory entity. This procedure requires several requirements such as a minimum age, a certain level of instruction, proof of financial knowledge, among others.

The job of a stockbroker is complex. It involves several essential components

Negotiate prices on behalf of your clients

Research the Stock Market for Sound Investments

Provide business advice to their clients

Give advice on opening and closing market prices

Explain investment options, benefits, and drawbacks to clients

You don't just pick up your mobile and shout "Buy! Sell !!" The normal thing is that you connect to the internet and register on the website of a broker, open an account with them (as if you opened it in a bank, the paperwork goes and returns by ordinary mail) and, from that website, you choose what you want to buy or sell and execute it all based on mouse clicks.

You can also use your **bank** as a **broker** service. That is, you can open a securities account with them and operate in the Stock Market from your bank. Although it is somewhat more expensive, **it is not a bad option for your first steps in the Stock Market**, because it saves you some initial difficulties.

For example, in a normal broker, you will have to open an account and put money in it, on the other hand, in the securities account that you open with your bank, the money can be taken directly from your checking account. Besides, most brokers do not have offices, or at least they do not have as much physical presence as your bank may have; And being able to talk to a real live person can help you a lot in the beginning.

Stockbrokers make the stock market accessible to almost everyone, regardless of budget, and even if investors are out of the country.

Broker services also increasingly include the use of roboadvisors. This makes the investment process even more agile. Roboadvisors is a system that uses algorithms to manage investments over the Internet. Roboadvisors are sometimes embedded in mobile phone applications. Roboadvisors allow the investment to be made with little or no human interaction. This also reduces transaction fees. The lack of the human element, however, leads to a decrease in personal service. Roboadvisors cannot provide the level of in-depth customer support that dedicated stockbrokers can.

To buy shares, you can do it at any time of the day if you do it via the web. However, your order will only be executed if the market is open (during business hours). If you place the order after hours, or even on a Sunday, it is stored and will be executed in the first minutes of the next trading day.

Finding the right broker for your business is key to making sound and smart investments. Stockbrokers are important professionals in the life of any growing business. Without brokers, entrepreneurs may be left with fewer options for growth. Here are 5 tips that you should use when you need a stockbroker;

Verify if they are Registered

First of all, it must be verified if the agent has the authorization to operate.

Don't rush the process finding the right broker can take time, but it is important to be thorough. Spending time with prospective stockbrokers is essential to determine if they have the proper knowledge and are trustworthy. This means that you will have to meet with the broker in question more than once.

- **Take your time when deciding**

Some brokers can be overly aggressive and try to rush potential clients into making investments Involved in Stock Trading.

FUNDAMENTAL ANALYSIS; STOCK TRADING

An organized market for justifiable items according to certain rules is called a stock exchange. For example, stocks, <u>bonds</u>, i.e. securities, or foreign exchange, and certain goods such as <u>raw materials can be</u> traded.

The stock exchange is the marketplace where supply and demand meet. The stock exchange connects shareholders who want to sell their shares with those investors who want to buy them. The marketplace also helps to determine a share price based on supply and demand. The exchange brings together supply and demand in line with the market and balances them out by setting prices. Here, supply and demand are determined by brokers during defined trading hours. In the case of <u>stock exchange trading, the</u> following applies: If there are more buy than sell requests (orders) for a share, the price of the share rises; if it is the other way around, it sinks.

Expectations and the fulfillment of expectations are of vital importance in the stock market. Often the stock exchange traders speculate on takeovers, sales of parts of the company, or mergers. If a rumor becomes a certainty, the prices change only rarely, even if it is very good or bad news, after all, the event is "priced in", as it is called in the stock market jargon.

Much more important is unexpected news. If, for example, the head of a company unexpectedly announces a slump in profits, improves the forecast for next year's business, or announces a revolutionary product, this often leads to price jumps. The same applies if a company significantly exceeds expectations.

At Apple, for example, when <u>Apple</u> boss Steve Jobs presented the first iPhone in 2007. From the point of view of that time, it was a revolutionary phone with many special functions such as a digital camera, computer functions, and music player in one. The customers and shareholders were impressed by the technology. The price rose strongly. At that time it was around 2.40 euros. Since then, the Apple share has been a guarantee of success and is now at 113 euros (as of February 8, 2021).

Likewise, bad news can depress a company's stock price. These ups and downs are characteristic of the stock market and are called volatility. Prices can fluctuate widely even within a day. Often, however, the price moves in the same direction over days or even weeks, sometimes even over several years. This movement is called a trend. If the prices of most stocks rise over a distinctly long period, the stock exchange traders speak of a **bull market**, and if prices fall, of a **bear market.**

Investors are especially afraid if prices fall rapidly across the board. Then one speaks of a **stock market crash.**

There are no stocks without risk. Neither dividends nor price increases are a sure source of profit. So only money should be used that is allowed to disappear if necessary. However, investors should bear in mind that in a time of zero interest rates, the money in the current, overnight, or savings account is "eaten up" by inflation. In other words: The money is safe in the bank, but always loses a little of its value due to the rising prices of living. There is the advised to have three net salaries in reserve to be able to pay rent, food, and transport if necessary.

Experts calculate a higher return on average for stocks, i.e. more profit, than for other investments. But factors such as investment volume - how much money can be invested - and time are also important. Also, what is true for stocks as a whole does not apply to every single stock. It is all the more important to be well informed when choosing stocks and to invest your money in various forms so that if you lose everything is not gone at once.

Why should you engage in stock trading?

The money that is invested in savings accounts is usually bombproof. However, if you have taken a look at the interest, you will know that this security is bought at the cost of very little increases in value and, in the worst case (inflation), even losses in value. But why should you still invest money in stocks when the risk is higher? Bonds also bring secure returns without too much risk.

In the past, however, investing in stocks (at least in the longer term) has always beaten other forms of investment such as bonds, savings accounts, etc.

When you trade stocks on the stock exchange, you can hope for profits from **price increases** and **dividend payments**. Dividends are part of the company's profits that some companies distribute to their shareholders. In this way, shareholders receive ongoing interest on their investment, even if they do not want to sell the shares. And if they do, they can benefit from the (hoped for) price increases through the sale. The higher profit expectations are of course bought with **higher risks**. In the event of a real stock market crash, the share price can drop by 50% or more.

However, with the right strategies, which you will learn about in this book, these risks can be minimized. You can even choose not to risk more than 1% of your market capital on any stock position.

Types of Stocks

There are different types of stocks or terms used to classify stocks. The types of shares. When looking for a broker, make it clear upfront that you are considering multiple brokers. No decision needs to be made on the spot, as you can always call back or meet again. Check if they are experienced, The longer the stockbroker has been in business, the greater his knowledge of the financial field. However, this is not a determining factor. It is also important to know how accurate the agent is in its market forecasts. The more successful you have been in the past, the more profit you will have generated for your customers.

- **Evaluate all your options**

Ask any questions you can think of, even if they seem basic. A good stockbroker will be happy to answer all of your questions to make sure you understand everything. The way a stockbroker answers your questions will tell you a lot about himself. If they rush you into a contract, can you continue to trust them once they get your money? A good sign is when a stockbroker opens the conversation by asking you what you want to know, rather than telling you what he wants you to hear.

- **Analyze if the price suits you**

Be sure to also ask how much brokers charge for transactions. This may seem awkward, but it is a business after all. You have the right to know how much you will be charged to invest. Many often do not give enough importance to the money they are going to pay in brokerage fees for products and services. Unfortunately, some riders are not frank at this point. Always keep it in mind. Good brokers are always honest with their clients.

- **Make sure you know which investments are right for you**

Most brokers receive a fixed percentage of your total account. In other words, your commission grows as your account does. Sometimes they also get additional compensation for recommending specific investments or funds offered by their company. However, your priority should be finding the most suitable investment for you. That means you have to find a broker who chooses the best investment, not the one that is supposed to sell you.

WAYS TO OPERATE ON STOCKS

The ways of operating on stocks are numerous, ranging from the classic purchase of corporate securities to the most modern derivative products.

CONVENTIONAL PURCHASE: When you buy shares in the conventional sense, you are buying a very small company. The more shares you have, the greater your stake in the company. Shares are traded in the thousands and many are being added or removed every day, but buying corporate securities is not for everyone and requires a significant outlay of money.

. These types of operations are usually carried out for long-term operations, in which a movement of months, years, or in some cases even decades in the price of the securities is expected. Such an investment is generally held for several Therefore, it is not the most suitable method to operate in the short term because it takes years, in some cases even decades, before the benefits materialize

When you own shares, you are also eligible to collect dividends (the number of profits that the company distributes to its shareholders). However, this is not an income stream that shareholders can rely on very much, since the decision on dividends is made exclusively by the management of the company.

Such investors are less sensitive to short-term fluctuations because they usually focus on fundamentals and long-term profit potential. Buying real stocks requires dealing with a stock market, and usually involves paying commissions. Another point to consider is the fact that profits from shares traded on a stock market are taxable. In

TRADING WITH CFDs: Contracts for Difference, also known as CFDs, solve the problem of the conventional way of investing in stocks. By not having to own the securities, the CFD allows us a total exposure to price movements, but without having to make a large outlay to acquire them in the property. Also, they are perfectly adapted to short and medium-term movements, also thanks to that facility provided by the low entry prices.

 STOCK MARKET FUTURES: Futures contracts are the most typical tool in commodity markets, especially those for crude oil and also for gold. However, they are not as common in the stock market. That does not mean that they are not used, despite everything, and they keep a great function as a derivative contract to operate long term. What makes the futures contract different from the CFD? Well, precisely because, due to the structure of commissions and initial payments, futures are better adapted to the long term and larger positions, while the opposite occurs with Contracts for Difference.

STOCK MARKET INDICES: The good thing about indices is that they allow us to bet on the price of the stock market, but not only on a title or security of a particular company but on those of an entire sector or country. Thus, we can open, for example, CFDs on the Ibex 35 (from the Madrid stock exchange), the Nasdaq 100, or the FTSE 100.

STOCK TRADING STRATEGIES

Buy and Hold

Buy and hold is about investing for the long term, which is different from pure stock trading, but because of its popularity and its efficiency, we have to take it into account.

Within this "Buy and Hold" we have a great variety of sub-systems.

We have the investment by value, by dividends, by momentum, by index.

All these variants have their defenders and detractors.

But the truth is that all of them behave under the same principle: which is to invest in the long term.

Depending on long-term trading cycles, some strategies will perform a little better than others, but in the end, there will be no significant differences.

In general, if you are a more conservative investor, a dividend strategy would suit you well.

On the contrary, if you are a more daring investor, you could try looking for momentum stocks, which are usually the hottest and most popular of the given moment.

Depending on when we buy or sell we will have a great variety in long-term returns.

Let's look at this illustration; We have two investors. Mr. X and Mr. Y

They both buy SpaceX shares to invest in the long term.

Mr. X bought in 2010 while Mr. Y who follows a value-type strategy decides not to buy on that date because he thinks SpaceX's price doesn't have much value (he thinks it is somewhat expensive).

One year later, Investor X has lost 30%, then Investor B decides that now there is value because the price has that 30% discount and buys. A year later that Mr. Y has gained 60%, Mr. X has just gained over 5%.

That is the difference in applying different purchasing strategies. This is not to say that investor B's strategy will always work well because on many occasions it happens that when "investor A" buys, the share price continues to rise non-stop for years.

Well, as we see this way of buying stocks to invest in the long term is very simple. We choose our preferred values, and then we decide if it is time to buy, and if we do we keep the investment for a period that is usually years. It is a good way to put savings in the long term, no doubt.

Position trading

This second way **is a kind of hybrid between investing (which we just saw) and short-term trading**. In this case, we hold the position for weeks, months, or even years, depending on each particular case. These types of trades **do not require trading very often**, so it is Ideal for most operators.

However, It is not recommended to those who have no experience in the markets because we have to know well what we are doing in terms of general risk and position.

Well, because in this strategy we have to pay attention to the long-term charts, and that means that we are going to try to operate the big stock trends, that will make us become more patient and meditate well on what we are going to do.

- **Overnight or after-hours trading**

Without being a way of trading different from the others in itself, it is another strategy that some people use, especially in the North American markets.

The characteristic of this type of trading is that traders start trading when the market is closed. As you should already know, the stock markets usually open in the morning and close in the afternoon. In the case of New York, that time is from 9:30 to 4:00 pm. As you can see, there are not many hours to negotiate that's just 6 and a half hours.

Hence it is not surprising that many people try to trade at times when the main market is closed. Those moments tend to be the ones with the most business and economic announcements, with sometimes wild movements.

There are people who prefer this type of trading because they can negotiate those economic announcements or they can find special opportunities. Likewise, many traders work during the day so they cannot trade during normal hours. This way they can trade after they get home from work. You also have to take into account **disadvantages such as** low liquidity and high spreads, <u>volatility</u>.

It is not a system that I like, nor do I use it in my strategies, but it is there for those who want to use it.

- **Day trading**

Here we come to the real monster of online trading.

Without a doubt, the most popular way of trading in the world, which does not mean that it is the best, at least for our pockets. Because it is in this style that it can be said that "95% of traders lose", so well known.

In Buy and Hold it is difficult to lose in the long term, although it is true that it is difficult to win a lot. In positional trading, you can lose but even doing it very badly takes a long time to do it.

However, in day trading it is not at all difficult to lose your shirt in just a few trading sessions. It is also true that it is easier to earn money quickly.

But the question here is whether we can maintain those profit ratios in the long term. The stock day trading market, as I said, is very popular. However, in my opinion, it is not as efficient as futures or even Forex or index CFDs could be.

These markets offer much more suitable volatility and trading costs for day traders. Stocks have greater problems to offer optimal conditions in day trading, since sometimes they do not move enough to justify the costs we pay, especially in the case of small speculators.

- **Scalping**

This way would become one of the variants of day trading, but since it is so popular I put it separately.

The key is to buy the stock at the right time, usually when the price is moving clearly in one direction, and close shortly after when we have accumulated a few profit points.

Many so-called industry experts try to attract the attention of stakeholders with typical claims that they can make $ 500 or $ 1,000 in a minute.

Unfortunately most of those who claim that are usually scammers who are looking to take advantage of inexperienced traders who believe these fairy tales.

What they do not tell you is that there is also a high probability that the price will turn around and move a few points against you, with which you would lose those 500 or 1,000 dollars plus the commission (and the spread).

Really, to win in this style of trading you need to be a true expert.

A **good way to try to learn to the scalp is in the Forex market**, where with micro-lots of 1,000 units we can make operations of 5 or 7 pips in a few minutes and see if the system is as easy as it seems.

That way you would only lose 0.5 euros or dollars per trade and it would not be as disastrous as losing 500.

Better yet, do it in demo mode so you don't risk anything. Although, there is nothing like doing it with real money.

- **Swing trading**

At last we come to the last form of stock trading.

Swing trading is the trading method that is between day trading and long-term investment.

That means that the positions will last for days, weeks, or months.

In many cases I can close up on the same day and in many others I let the operation run for months.

The advantage of this system?

Above all, it allows you to take advantage of the long-term trends of the markets, both bullish and bearish.

This is very difficult to achieve in day trading.

On the contrary, long-term investment is the best to find these trends, but if security is very volatile, we will be losing a large number of opportunities, which is not the case with swing trading, which always allows us to re-enter operations when the price moves to one side of the market significantly.

As for leverage, it is a system in which we can use as much power as day trading since I do not hesitate to use almost 5: 1 at times. Something that we cannot do in long-term investing, where we have to go with 1: 1 leverage.

Another advantage, especially with day trading, is that **trading costs are less important** because we are looking for wide movements, of 5, 10, 15% or more.

If the total cost of the operation is 0.2%, it is not significant if we look for movements of 10%.

Now, if we do day trading and look for a 1% movement, that 0.2% does become significant and in the long run, it will weigh like a slab in our trading.

We can bet in favor of the trend or we can bet contrary that it ends.

I already told you that you will do better to go looking for the main trend, whether it is bullish or bearish. Opposing the market tends to pay dearly in the long run. To swing trading the other way around, you have to be a very experienced speculator with a refined technique. It costs to reach it. But when it's done it's worth it.

Buy and Hold

Buy and hold is about investing for the long term,

which is different from pure stock trading, but because of its popularity and its efficiency, we have to take it into account.

Within this "Buy and Hold" we have a great variety of sub-systems.

We have the investment by value, by dividends, by momentum, by index.

All these variants have their defenders and detractors.

But the truth is that all of them behave under the same principle: which is to invest in the long term.

Depending on long-term trading cycles, some strategies will perform a little better than others, but in the end, there will be no significant differences.

In general, if you are a more conservative investor, a dividend strategy would suit you well.

On the contrary, if you are a more daring investor, you could try looking for momentum stocks, which are usually the hottest and most popular of the given moment.

Depending on when we buy or sell we will have a great variety in long-term returns.

Let's look at this illustration; We have two investors. Mr. X and Mr. Y

They both buy SpaceX shares to invest in the long term.

Mr. X bought in 2010 while Mr. Y who follows a value-type strategy decides not to buy on that date because he thinks SpaceX's price doesn't have much value (he thinks it is somewhat expensive).

One year later, Investor X has lost 30%, then Investor B decides that now there is value because the price has that 30% discount and buys. A year later that Mr. Y has gained 60%, Mr. X has just gained over 5%.

That is the difference in applying different purchasing strategies. This is not to say that investor B's strategy will always work well because on many occasions it happens that when "investor A" buys, the share price continues to rise non-stop for years.

Well, as we see this way of buying stocks to invest in the long term is very simple. We choose our preferred values, and then we decide if it is time to buy, and if we do we keep the investment for a period that is usually years. It is a good way to put savings in the long term, no doubt.

Position trading

This second way **is a kind of hybrid between investing (which we just saw) and short-term trading**. In this case, we hold the position for weeks, months, or even years, depending on each particular case. These types of trades **do not require trading very often**, so it is Ideal for most operators.

However, It is not recommended to those who have no experience in the markets because we have to know well what we are doing in terms of general risk and position.

Well, because in this strategy we have to pay attention to the long-term charts, and that means that we are going to try to operate the big stock trends, that will make us become more patient and meditate well on what we are going to do.

Overnight or after-hours trading

Without being a way of trading different from the others in itself, it is another strategy that some people use, especially in the North American markets.

The characteristic of this type of trading is that traders start trading when the market is closed. As you should already know, the stock markets usually open in the morning and close in the afternoon. In the case of New York, that time is from 9:30 to 4:00 pm. As you can see, there are not many hours to negotiate that's just 6 and a half hours.

Hence it is not surprising that many people try to trade at times when the main market is closed. Those moments tend to be the ones with the most business and economic announcements, with sometimes wild movements.

Some people prefer this type of trading because they can negotiate those economic announcements or they can find special opportunities. Likewise, many traders work during the day so they cannot trade during normal hours. This way they can trade after they get home from work. You also have to take into account **disadvantages such as** low liquidity and high spreads, <u>volatility</u>.

It is not a system that I like, nor do I use it in my strategies, but it is there for those who want to use it.

Day trading

Here we come to the real monster of online trading.

Without a doubt, the most popular way of trading in the world, which does not mean that it is the best, at least for our pockets. Because it is in this style that it can be said that "<u>95% of traders lose</u>", so well known.

In Buy and Hold it is difficult to lose in the long term, although it is true that it is difficult to win a lot. In positional trading, you can lose but even doing it very badly takes a long time to do it.

However, in day trading it is not at all difficult to lose your shirt in just a few trading sessions. It is also true that it is easier to earn money quickly.

But the question here is whether we can maintain those profit ratios in the long term. The stock day trading market, as I said, is very popular. However, in my opinion, it is not as efficient as futures or even Forex or index CFDs could be.

These markets offer much more suitable volatility and trading costs for day traders. Stocks have greater problems to offer optimal conditions in day trading, since sometimes they do not move enough to justify the costs we pay, especially in the case of small speculators.

Scalping

This way would become one of the variants of day trading, but since it is so popular I put it separately.

The key is to buy the stock at the right time, usually when the price is moving clearly in one direction, and close shortly after when we have accumulated a few profit points.

Many so-called industry experts try to attract the attention of stakeholders with typical claims that they can make $ 500 or $ 1,000 in a minute.

Unfortunately, most of those who claim that are usually scammers who are looking to take advantage of inexperienced traders who believe these fairy tales.

What they do not tell you is that there is also a high probability that the price will turn around and move a few points against you, with which you would lose those 500 or 1,000 dollars plus the commission (and the spread).

To win in this style of trading you need to be a true expert.

A good way to try to learn to the scalp is in the Forex market, where with micro-lots of 1,000 units we can make operations of 5 or 7 pips in a few minutes and see if the system is as easy as it seems.

That way you would only lose 0.5 euros or dollars per trade and it would not be as disastrous as losing 500.

Better yet, do it in demo mode so you don't risk anything. Although, there is nothing like doing it with real money.

Swing trading

At last, we come to the last form of stock trading.

Swing trading is the trading method that is between day trading and long-term investment.

That means that the positions will last for days, weeks, or months.

In many cases, I can close up on the same day and in many others I let the operation run for months.

The advantage of this system?

Above all, it allows you to take advantage of the long-term trends of the markets, both bullish and bearish.

This is very difficult to achieve in day trading.

On the contrary, long-term investment is the best to find these trends, but if security is very volatile, we will be losing a large number of opportunities, which is not the case with swing trading, which always allows us to re-enter operations when the price moves to one side of the market significantly.

As for leverage, it is a system in which we can use as much power as day trading since I do not hesitate to use almost 5: 1 at times. Something that we cannot do in long-term investing, where we have to go with 1: 1 leverage.

Another advantage, especially with day trading, is that **trading costs are less important** because we are looking for wide movements, of 5, 10, 15% or more.

If the total cost of the operation is 0.2%, it is not significant if we look for movements of 10%.

Now, if we do day trading and look for a 1% movement, that 0.2% does become significant and in the long run, it will weigh like a slab in our trading.

We can bet in favor of the trend or we can bet contrary that it ends.

I already told you that you will do better to go looking for the main trend, whether it is bullish or bearish. Opposing the market tends to pay dearly in the long run. To swing trading the other way around, you have to be a very experienced speculator with a refined technique. It costs to reach it. But when it's done it's worth it

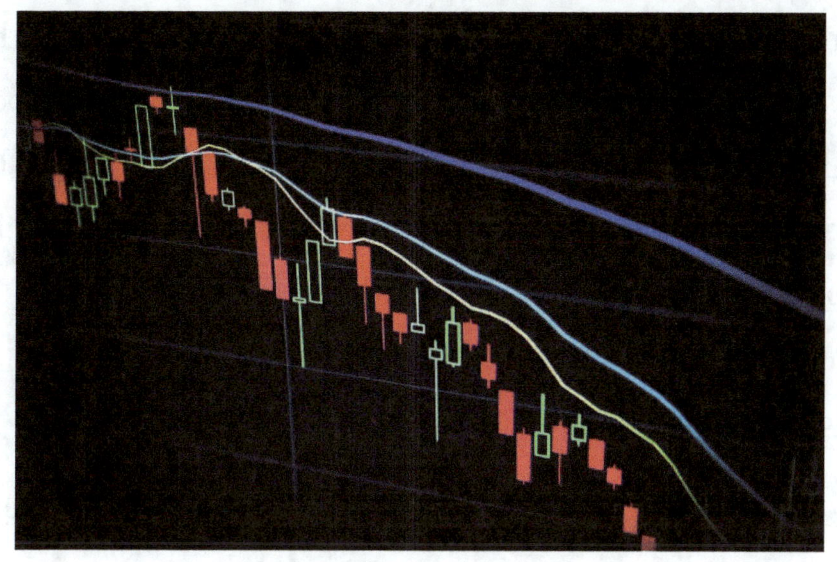

INVESTMENT STRATEGIES

In the long term, you can usually only be successful on the stock market with a strong investment strategy. Before starting the stock market as a beginner, it is therefore important to find a proven stock market strategy.

Here are a few tips on investment strategy

Almost every stock market strategy is better than buying blindly at will. It is therefore important to implement a stock market strategy 1 to 1, otherwise the risk of loss increases. The great advantage of stock market strategies is that you can hardly or not at all be guided by emotional (wrong) decisions. Because as soon as emotions are involved, it often goes wrong on the stock market and leads to losses (see also <u>risk stocks</u>).

A basic distinction is made between an active and a passive approach in stock exchange strategies (detailed information: <u>invest actively or passively?</u>) an active strategy aims to beat the major <u>indices</u> by buying selected stocks and thus achieve a better result and thus a higher return than, for example, the <u>DAX</u> and <u>Dow Jones</u>. Alternatively, using a passive investment method, you can simply replicate the DAX and Co. 1 to 1 with <u>index funds or ETFs</u> and not even try to beat the market. Such an overall market investment strategy can be implemented with relatively little effort (very easily, for example, with a <u>savings plan</u>).

Stock exchange strategies differ primarily based on the type of <u>stock analysis</u> and its numerous analysis options. Usually, these are <u>fundamental analysis</u> on the one hand and <u>technical analysis</u> on the other. These analysis methods usually play a decisive role, especially with active equity strategies. But the passive investment approach, too, is often based on data from fundamental and/or technical analysis.

There are investment strategies that are easy to implement and are therefore also suitable for beginners (such as the passive approach just mentioned). And those that are more difficult to implement (various active strategies, for example, are more suitable for advanced and professionals). Depending on the type of strategy, you need more or less time, which you have to invest overall. It is also important to consider the risk: there are riskier strategies and less risky ones.

If possible, check whether the selected stock exchange strategy has proven itself over the long term (this is easy with a passive approach, as you only have to look at the long-term <u>charts of</u> the preferred <u>indices</u>). But remember one way or another, success in the past can never guarantee success in the future.

During the <u>financial crisis</u> or other economic crises, some active Stock market strategies were badly damaged. Therefore, one should choose an exchange strategy that has weathered past crises relatively well (= did not perform worse than the <u>overall market</u>). In times of acute crisis, it also makes less sense to start an investment strategy. Then it is better to wait until the stock market situation has stabilized again to some extent.

Risks involved in investing in Stock Market.

Investing in the stock market always involves a series of **risks that we must take into account** before buying shares. Here we analyze the main **risks when investing in the stock market**: market risk, currency risk, or liquidity risk. What risks do I face when investing my money?

Main risks that we can find when investing in the stock market

Market risk (also known as systematic risk)

This is the **risk that investors run of suffering variations in the price of our financial products**, such as stocks or bonds. This is the probability that we have of **losing part of the purchase value of**, for example, the shares of a company, when the market experiences a decline. Other aspects such as the **variability and volatility faced by the market**, as well as the relationship with economic cycles, come into play in this risk. This type of risk is the broadest and covers all **financial assets**: both bonds, funds, stocks, and other investment products.

To try to **minimize this market risk, it is very important to diversify your investment portfolio**. With this, you will avoid that, even though a certain share or financial asset in your portfolio suffers a decrease, you do not lose all the value of the portfolio and this decrease can be compensated with other acquired securities that are on the rise.

Liquidity risk

This risk can occur when you want to sell or liquidate a position at certain security. This **can happen since at the moment it may be the case that there are no buyers for that security**, and the lack of liquidity in the market forces us to sell at a lower price. Therefore, when investing **we must look at the capitalization of the company** since it is not the same to invest in a large capitalization company as in a company with a low capitalization: the former will always have less liquidity risk. We must also look at the company's price range, which will indicate its degree of liquidity.

Unsystematic risk

By non-systematic risk we understand that **particular risk of each company**, that is, the risk resulting from **factors specific to each company**. This type of risk affects only the company itself, not the rest of the market. This risk is usually said to be diversifiable because there is the possibility of reducing or controlling it through adequate diversification, diversification aimed at achieving an optimal portfolio of securities.

To avoid this, it is always advisable to study the company in depth before investing and value it against the competition, the sector, and the market.

Operational risk

It covers **all those financial losses suffered by a listed company**, **caused by failures** or deficiencies that processes, people, technology, internal systems, etc ... may suffer.

This type of risk does not take into account losses caused by changes in the political, economic, and social environment, since they are factors external to the company itself. An example of operational risk can be, for example, a flash crash due to human error or a computer algorithm (HFT).

To avoid this, we can look at the measures that companies take to control and avoid operational problems that may affect the proper functioning of their activity.

Counterparty risk

This risk **arises when one of the parties fulfills its obligation in the sale and the other party does not do so simultaneously**. It is eliminated from operations carried out through an organized market. In the case of derivatives, it is avoided by having a clearinghouse (Clearing House): this solution is not so easy to carry out given the complexity of the liquidation operations of the stock markets, especially in the OTC markets (not organized).

Currency risk

This risk appears when you **invest in a currency other than yours**: by changing the type of currency you may suffer a variation or devaluation of the issuing currency and lose part of the value of your investment. This is the case of investing in US stocks: if you invest in dollars, it will be beneficial for you if the euro rises against the dollar and vice versa if you are interested in selling your shares.

Legislative risk

This type of risk **does not depend directly on the market but depends on the authority** that Congress has to change or create laws that may affect certain sectors or the market in general. Pending laws that when enacted may negatively affect the previously selected value should always be taken into account before investing.

Price risk

It is one of the risks that the investor usually takes into account more since a decrease in the price can cause their investment to lose value. Mainly the price of an investment is reflected through the different factors that affect supply and demand.

Inflation risk

It is one of the most prominent risks among investors since **if the inflation rate is higher than the return generated by our investment, the money invested will have a lower purchasing power**, and therefore we will find a negative real return. In other words, inflation reduces the return that an investment generates, although historically stocks have remained ahead of inflation.

Interest risk

This affects the **sensitivity of your investments to possible changes in interest rates**. Mainly this risk affects investments that offer fixed income, such as bonds and preferred shares, but also to indebted companies since a variation in the interest rate will vary the amount to be paid.

DANGERS OF STOCK TRADING

It is important to keep the risk involved in trading stocks and other securities in mind as a beginner. When it comes to stocks and the stock market, however, many investors primarily think of profit opportunities. Unfortunately, the numerous risks of loss are quickly forgotten, especially when high returns are in prospect. The good news is that most risks are relatively easy to avoid. You just have to know them:

Here are few dangers on the stock market and how to avoid them

DANGER 1:

You have no investment strategy and haphazardly buy stocks that you find interesting from the gut.

Without a strong equity strategy, it is very difficult to be successful in the stock market. Also, betting on no strategy or the wrong strategy can have serious consequences (see some of the following hazards as examples).

DANGER 2:

You do not use stop prices when trading stocks.

Many inexperienced newcomers make this mistake. Please make sure to use stop prices when trading on the stock exchange to automatically avoid larger losses. Using stops is very easy. You just have to know how it works.

Many private investors do not use stops and so may lose a lot of money in the event of a sharp price slide. Especially in times of crisis, countless shareholders have suffered major losses by not using stop prices. Always Put stops to hedge your stocks.

DANGER 3:

One can be tempted by dubious stock tips to buy bad stocks.

An incredibly important topic on the stock market! Black sheep in the financial sector tries to rip off naive investors time and again. Many inexperienced investors have already lost a lot of money this way. Beware of these shares buy recommendations

DANGER 4:

You only invest the money in 1 or 2 stocks (or other securities).

Don't do that! Because this increases the risk of making losses and not making money with stocks. Instead, buy at least 10 different stocks. This is how you split the risk across several stocks. The best way to illustrate this is with a simple example:

Case 1: Mr. X buys only one share for 30,000 euros (share 1). In the following weeks, this share 1 fell by 20%. Consequence: Mr. X. made a loss of 6000 euros.

Case 2: Mr. Y also invested 30,000 euros in shares at the same time. But Mr. Y used the money to buy 3 different shares at EUR 10,000 each (share 1, share 2 and share 3). The development of the shares could then have gone something like this:

Share 1: -20% (= € 2,000 loss with a stake of € 10,000)

Stock 2: + 10% (= gain € 1,000 in a stake of € 10,000)

Stock 3: + 20% (= gain € 2,000 in a stake of € 10,000)

That means, Mr. B. made a total profit of 1,000 euros with 30,000 euros because he invested his money in 3 different stocks. Mr. A., on the other hand, is sitting on a loss of 6000 euros because he only invested all his money in one share. There are of course times when the stock market is doing badly and many stocks are falling, then there are also less <u>promising stocks</u> to buy. At such times it can make perfect sense to own only 1 or 2 shares (or none at all) and instead focus more on cash or other safer securities.

DANGER 5:

You think that you can be successful on the stock market with almost no knowledge of the stock market.

Or maybe you even think that as a beginner you can make a lot of money quickly with stocks? My advice: Say goodbye to this wishful thinking. Do not let greed for stock gains get out of hand and so tempt you to rush to buy stocks. That has already broken the necks of many private investors.

Instead, take time to educate yourself. For example, in books like this. It is also sensible to practice stock trading risk-free using a model portfolio with play money before getting started

DANGER 6:

As a beginner, trade dangerous derivatives such as warrants, leverage certificates, Forex, or CFDs.

The risk of loss with these financial instruments is a lot higher! Due to the increased risk, leveraged forms of investment can also be used to achieve higher profits more quickly. But the price for this is a significantly increased risk of loss. <u>CFD trading in</u> particular is extremely dangerous, The same goes for <u>Forex trading</u>. Therefore, as a beginner, you should stay away from the vast majority of <u>derivatives</u> and concentrate better on less risky financial stocks such as stocks and/or funds.

DANGER 7:

As a newcomer to stocks, you only get in at low prices because you think you are getting a "bargain".

It is believed that high profits can be achieved with stocks when buying at a low price (in other words: the stock is currently at a price low and was significantly higher some time ago). Do not reach into falling knives, as an old stock market adage says. Because the risk of further falling prices is often high.

DANGER 8:

People are rashly buying and selling stocks all the time (for whatever reason).

The stock should be given time to develop (unless it is stopped out, see DANGER 2). It is well known that patience often pays off. Another disadvantage with frequent purchases and sales: High broker trading costs, as you have to pay fees with every transaction.

DANGER 9:

You only invest in very cheap stocks (= penny stocks).

Stay away from <u>Pennystock stocks</u>! There are certainly a few interesting penny stocks. But often there are junk stocks or stock corporations behind it that are worth almost nothing and are on the verge of bankruptcy. Just because a stock appears cheap in terms of price doesn't mean it is cheap. It depends on the development of the percent share.

Penny stock trading is only for risk-taking and more experienced stock gamblers who hope that the stock may rise again after all (mostly short-term, if at all). Particularly dangerous penny stocks are <u>occasionally</u> advertised in <u>dubious stock</u> recommendations.

DANGER 10:

If you are in the plus, you get out too early.

I and many stock market experts recommend that you let profits run and only get out when the upward trend is reversed. True to the motto: *"The trend is your friend"*

DANGER 11:

You do not want to realize losses.

It is difficult to sell a stock that has been in the red for a long time: If a stock continues to fall further and further, then many have the hope that the stock will rise again soon. These investors are holding on to the stock and waiting for better times. But sometimes these better times don't come. Consequence: The losses keep getting bigger.

DANGER 12:

Buy stocks with a loan or trade securities with the money you need to live.

Don't take out a loan to have money to buy stocks (regardless of where the loan is coming from). This increases the risk of going into debt even more if prices fall. Besides, the interest on a bank loan hurts even more if you speculate. Rule: Only buy stocks with your own money!

Also only deal with money that you do not need to live and where you can cope with a total loss if necessary.

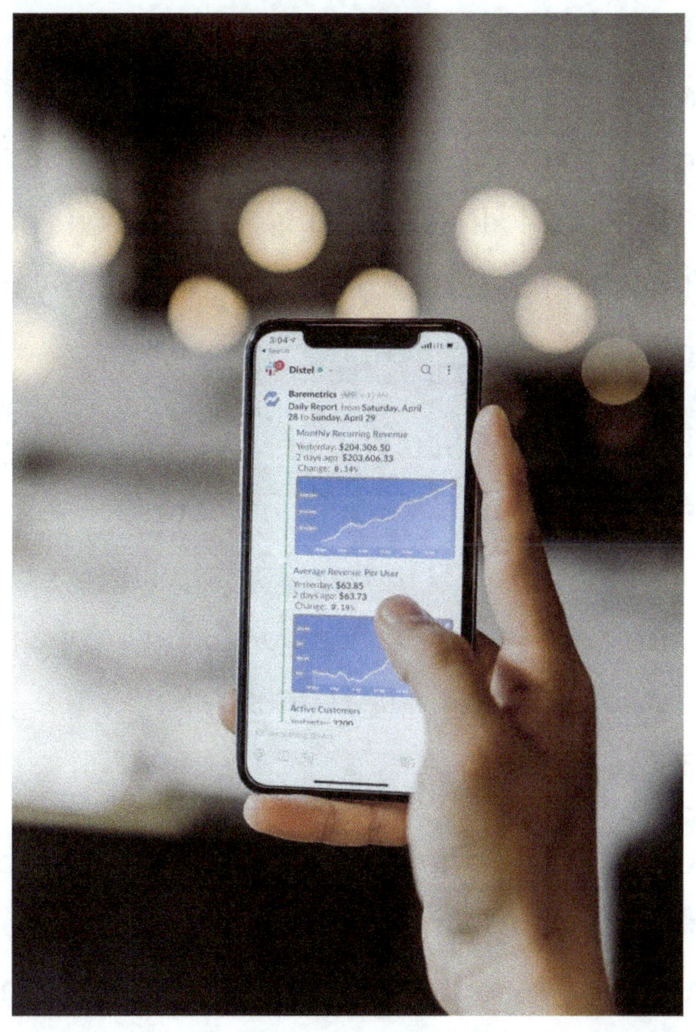

TRADING PSYCHOLOGY

Stock market psychology is a branch of financial psychology and revolves around the

mood and behavior of investors on the stock market. Because stock market prices are strongly influenced by the unpredictable psychology of investors. Above all, fear of (loss) and greed (profit) is pronounced on the stock market and regularly leads to numerous bad investment decisions.

The stock market reacts to just 10 percent. Everything else is psychology!" This is of course a bit of an exaggeration. But Trading psychology plays an important part in investment decisions, especially in hectic (<u>stock market crash</u>) times

Intuitive human traits like cognitive biases and emotions play an important role in trading psychology. The main focus in learning about trading psychology is to become aware of the various pitfalls associated with a negative psychological trait and to develop more positive personality traits. Traders who are well versed in trading psychology generally do not act out of cognitive biases or emotions. They, therefore, have greater chances of making a profit or at least minimizing their losses in their market activities.

Trading psychology raises the following questions: How do investors react psychologically to certain situations and information ... and why? How are investment behavior and thus investment decisions influenced from a psychological point of view?

Trading psychology differs from trader to trader, as influencing factors such as one's own emotions and predetermined cognitive distortions affect the individual. All of these emotions can lead to hasty and bad trading in the stock market. Many stock market dangers are therefore related to stock market psychology.

Some emotions that can affect trading are:

satisfaction

impatience

Anger

anxiety

Pride

Greed

As I said, psychology influences the development of stock prices. Certain moods among investors can lead to exaggerations more or less quickly. Above all fear plays a major role in the stock market, especially in times of crisis. It is not uncommon for fear to induce investors to make unreasonable decisions. Investment decisions are then made out of fear that does not make sense at all.

The more psychologically vulnerable you are, the more difficult it is often to be successful in the stock market. But there are ways to fight it and thus better control the emotions that are dangerous to the stock market (because you can hardly turn them off completely).

HOW TO IMPROVE YOUR TRADING PSYCHOLOGY

The easiest way to improve your trading psychology is to learn about your own emotions, cognitive biases, and personality traits. Once you have accepted these, you can develop your trading plan that takes these factors into account in hopes of reducing the impact of these traits on your decision-making.

For example, if you are a fundamentally confident person, you may find that overconfidence and pride affect your decision-making. An example: You do not intervene in the event of losses in the hope of a market turnaround, instead of accepting a small loss. This can result in even higher losses or even ruin your trading account.

To counteract this, you can set stops before opening the position to minimize your losses and decide when to close a particular trade. In doing so, you have visualized your cognitive distortions and emotions and made the conscious decision not to let them guide you. Instead, you have taken active steps against it.

How do cognitive biases affect trading?

Cognitive biases interfere with the trading process because, by definition, they are a predetermined personal propensity for or against something. As a result, your decision-making in your market activities is compromised as your judgment is clouded and you rely on gut instinct rather than sound fundamental or technical analysis.

The reason for this is to be found in the trading distortion. This means that you are more likely to trade an asset that you have successfully traded in the past or to avoid an asset on which you have suffered a historical loss. A trader needs to understand their distortions. This can help overcome this and lead to a more rational approach to the market and a more nuanced mindset.

There are five main types of cognitive bias:

1. **Representative bias** means that you are clinging to, or trying to copy, previously successful trades. They don't even do any analysis on the trades as they have proven themselves in the past. However, even with similar trades, it is important to approach each trade for its worth, not its past success

2. **Negative bias** leads to only looking at the negative sides of a trade rather than the good sides. This can mean that you overturn an entire strategy and only had to tweak a few tweaks to make a profit.

3. The **status quo bias** suggests that instead of trying something new, you're sticking to your old strategies or doing proven trades - you're stuck with the status quo. The danger arises from incorrectly assessing whether the tried and tested methods can still be implemented in the current market.

4. In the case of **confirmation bias**, you only look for the news and analyzes that confirm your pre-formulated ideas, or give them more weight. It is also

possible that they do not search for information at all or ignore information that contradicts their beliefs.

5. In the **gambler's fallacy**, you assume that a rising asset will continue to rise. But there is no reason to believe. Similar to the fact that there is no reason for a coin to always land number up instead of its head after successfully doing it a few times in a row.

SEVEN TIPS FOR AVOIDING EMOTION-LED TRADING

1. Identify your personality traits

2. Develop a trading plan and stick to it

3. Be patient

4. Be adaptable

5. Take a break after a loss

6. Accept your winnings

7. Keep a trading log

Identify your personality traits

One of the most important aspects of developing successful trading psychology is that you determine your personality traits at the beginning. In doing so, you have to be honest with yourself and admit to yourself, for example, that you have impulsive tendencies or tend to act out of anger and frustration.

If so, you need to keep these personality traits under control while you are active in the market. Because these characteristics can lead to a rash or imprudent decision without an analytical background. However, it is also important to play out your strengths. For example, if you are of a calm or calculative manner, you can benefit from this personal trait in your market activities.

Just as important as recognizing and knowing your personality traits and emotions is recognizing the personal biases mentioned above. Cognitive biases are an innate aspect of human nature. Before opening or closing a trade, you should understand your individual biases.

Develop a trading plan and stick to it

Developing a trading plan is critical to achieving your goals. A trading plan serves as a blueprint for your trading activity. In it, you determine your time commitment, available trading resources, the risk-reward ratio, and a trading strategy with which you are familiar.

For example, you can specify in a trading plan that you spend an hour trading in the morning and evening and never spend more than 2% of your total portfolio value on a trade. This practice can help minimize losses and limit the impact of emotion on your trading, as you have already established the rules for opening or closing a position.

When creating a trading plan, you should also consider individual factors such as emotions, personal biases, and personality traits that can affect your trading discipline. If you consider your personal biases before you start trading, you may be less likely to be guided by them.

Be patient

Patience is an essential part of discipline. It is therefore crucial that you remain patient with your positions. Trading out of emotion can result in missing out on a profit by closing a position too early. Trust your analysis and be patient and disciplined. It is also important to be patient and wait for an opportune moment to enter a trade, rather than rushing straight into it.

Be adaptable

While a trading plan is very important, always remember that no two trading days are the same. And there are no streaks of luck in stock trading either. With this in mind, it should be easy for you to assess and adjust to different sentiments in the market from day today.

If the market is very volatile on a day compared to the previous day and the market development is not exactly clear, it sometimes makes sense to let trading activity sit for a long time until you understand what is going on in the markets. Being adaptable can also help rule out emotions and representative and status quo biases. This will put you in a position to evaluate each situation in terms of your own merits. Another positive side effect of this ability is that it ensures that you act pragmatically when you are active in the markets.

Take a break after a loss

Sometimes after a loss, it is best to let your trading account sit idle for a while, rearrange your thoughts and calm down, rather than throwing yourself into the next trade and trying to recoup the losses.

The best traders are those who take their losses and see them as a learning opportunity. They usually take a few minutes before continuing trading. You use the time to analyze what went wrong in a particular trade and hope to avoid this mistake in the future.

This way they can keep their emotions like pride or fear under control before moving on to the next trade. This cool-down phase ensures a clear head and ensures a reliable assessment.

Accept your winnings

Even after you've made a profit, taking a break is usually a good idea. With multiple wins or a particularly high win, you can quickly think of yourself as invincible. The result: they throw you into another position and try to repeat your success.

You may even start several new positions and believe none of them will disappoint because today is "Your Day". This means you take unnecessary risks and diversify your portfolio far too quickly without a thorough analysis of the relevant markets.

So satisfaction can be just as dangerous for your market activities as anger. It is therefore important that you recognize when your decision-making is impaired or adversely affecting your trading psychology.

Keep a trading log

With a trading log, you record all losses and gains as well as the emotions experienced. Therefore, it is the culmination of all of the points mentioned earlier in this article. It can be used to assess whether your decision was the right one at a certain point in time or not.

For example, you can record the point in time when you decided to limit your losses, as well as the final price that the asset ultimately reached. From this, you can see if you made the right decision or not. You can also note when you booked your profits and whether your decision to close the position too early or too late was guided by your emotions.

WAYS TO BE PSYCHOLOGY FIT

Free yourself from fear and greed

There are always reasons to buy or sell stocks. Greed for more money when things go well, Fear of losing even more money if things go bad. Fear of missing exit times or opportunities. The need to right often obstruct the view of reality. Greed eats the brain; Fear eats the brain. And the desire to show everyone else too.

If you let yourself be guided by these feelings - consciously or unconsciously - when investing, you also have a lot of work to do. He is forced to put his investment decisions to the test every day, to weigh them up against the investment universe out there. They say investing is hard work but that's not true Investing is just no work - if you stay calm and are satisfied with swimming with the market.

Split your money

No investment is without risk. If you want to achieve a return that is above the interest rate for overnight money, you also have to be prepared to take the corresponding risks.

Everything has its price on the financial market - higher return opportunities mean higher risks, and more security is paid for with lower interest rates with one exception: Those who divide their money into different asset classes receive more security at no additional cost.

Don't fall in love - invest broadly

With so much sober consideration, the investor could easily lose the fun of it. Note costs. Taming feelings. Don't dare to bet.

But the use of such bets should be expendable "play money" and not a component of the retirement provision.

With this sober topic, gambling and any kind of emotional fluctuations should be avoided as far as possible: Instead of falling in love with individual stocks and, if necessary, defending them against the rest of the world, one should rather rely on the entire investment world.

A passive index fund on a global index like the MSCI World is not an investment with which one can amaze friends. "Nevertheless, you can invest in several hundred companies worldwide in one fell swoop," says Weber.

If, on the other hand, you try to achieve the necessary widespread over the selection of 50 to 60 individual titles, you will inevitably end up in the cost trap. A passive index or sector fund is less sporty, but sensible.

Nevertheless, there is no "right" or "wrong" depot. The decision as to how much risk one can take remains individual - because possible profit and the risk of losses belong together. For a successful investment, you need a meaningful concept and, quite simply, luck.

On the other hand, you don't need a gut feeling for the "right" systems

Set an investment horizon

Be clear about what your investment horizon is. If you have an investment horizon of ten or 15 years, you usually don't have to worry about making up for losses that have occurred in the meantime.

Prepare an exit strategy

Don't just think about the good times in the stock market. Think about what to do if there is turmoil on the stock exchanges. It helps to set clear guidelines beforehand. Do I stay firmly invested despite the stock market thunderstorm or do I get out when things get restless? With the latter, you should determine in advance when you will get off. With losses of ten percent? Or 15 percent? Anyone who thinks about this before the crisis acts less in an effect.

Trading psychology in a nutshell

Trading psychology is all about your mindset when you are active in the markets. This can be used to find explanations for your gains or losses.

It is important to understand your weaknesses and cognitive biases before opening a position. At the same time, you have to know your strengths very well

Learn from your wins and losses, but always remember: there are no winning streaks in trading, and each position should be evaluated in terms of its values

Knowing when to make a profit and when to limit a loss is what makes the difference between a good day in the markets and a bad day

Keep a trading log to check what worked and what didn't, and whether, at any given point in time, your decision was the right one. Use this information to improve your decision-making in the future

www.ingramcontent.com/pod-product-compliance
Lightning Source LLC
LaVergne TN
LVHW020608200726
843509LV00001B/19